Celtic Ripples

SEÁN FRANCIS MARTIN O'DONOGHUE

TRAFFORD
PUBLISHING

The picture on the front cover depicts a diver working at 125ft with a Unit of Radiography, Non Destuctive Testing (N.D.T.) equipment on the Claymore Alpha Oil Rig in the North Sea.

Note for Librarians: A cataloguing record for this book is available from Library and Archives Canada at www.collectionscanada.ca/amicus/index-e.html
ISBN 1-4120-5580-6

Trafford's print shop runs on "green energy" from solar, wind and other environmentally-friendly power sources.

Offices in Canada, USA, Ireland and UK
This book was published *on-demand* in cooperation with Trafford Publishing. On-demand publishing is a unique process and service of making a book available for retail sale to the public taking advantage of on-demand manufacturing and Internet marketing. On-demand publishing includes promotions, retail sales, manufacturing, order fulfilment, accounting and collecting royalties on behalf of the author.

Book sales for North America and international:
Trafford Publishing, 6E–2333 Government St.,
Victoria, BC v8t 4p4 CANADA
phone 250 383 6864 (toll-free 1 888 232 4444)
fax 250 383 6804; email to orders@trafford.com
Book sales in Europe:
Trafford Publishing (uk) Limited, 9 Park End Street, 2nd Floor
Oxford, UK oxi 1hh UNITED KINGDOM
phone 44 (0)1865 722 113 (local rate 0845 230 9601)
facsimile 44 (0)1865 722 868; info.uk@trafford.com
Order online at:
trafford.com/05-0478

10 9 8 7 6 5 4 3

Introduction

When you've rambled and roved and worked and loved in many places for many years, your mind is filled with thoughts and memories, which you need to reveal. I have put these thoughts and memories into prose and song and verse and I hope the reader will enjoy.

Seán O'Donoghue
Email: seanfmodonoghue@yahoo.ie

A creative writer on tour with *Celtic Ripples* the book.

Celtic Ripples – the list so far. By way of introduction: Seán has had 64 jobs in 17 countries with 37 changes of address, 39 girlfriends, 25 nervous breakdowns and 22 cars. The following are a list of completed works to date:

Short Story
Ripples Public Speaker of the Year Award, 1992, Scotland.

Drama
The Rosary Beads, a peace play about Ulster. Aberdeen Arts Festival, Spring, 1992.

Music
The Seven Flowers of Ballymun, an ecological view of the regeneration of North Dublin's Ballymun flats.

Poetry Book
Celtic Ripples

Autobiographical work in Progress
You Butterfly, You Know Good

Contents

They Made the Time to Listen.

For all the people who listened; my mother and father, my siblings, doctors, nurses, taxi drivers and Vasil.

There are times when men need listening to
A need so great that if you knew
How much it means to pass it on
Those feelings that come from the days that are gone

Sometimes a man unburdens
Just a little of his day
Then he walks into his world again lighter on his way.

Yes! A listener does a healing like no one else can do.
That's why I've put these words down
Especially for you.

Mariska

A young Polish girl came to work with us in Albany Life Assurance Co. She didn't stay long as the job was commission only, but she put a huge amount of effort in, which I recognised.

We were privileged and pleased to have her break
through the gentle draught that lay employed
outside the office door,
And to listen to her laughter cascade around the room
and over the wooden desk.
To daily watch her task herself against the phone and
learn new facts fast to combat dreaded rejection.
In the evening she would move, granite block by
grey granite block, towards her quarry
And in the morning her laughter starts another day.
We smile, she learns the Irish way.

Two Towers

Written in Sandymount, Dublin 1994.
Dedicated to Joanne.

Two towers alone
In the sky at night
One without and one with light
They stand alone both straight and high.
Two of them reaching
For the sky.

They maintain their interval so much
Sometimes I wish that they could touch.

Conform

Conform! The cry came from the west

Conform you say, I'll do my best

Too late, too late, the seeds are sown

I'll conform to standards of my own.

Alone in a Diving Bell

Bell-diving on the Moray Harstad, 1993.

Dressed head to toe in rubber
Surrounded by white light
Metal tubes, gauges and
My bell-partner's umbilical.

Black fins caress the ocean
As through the open hatch
I listen to the working breath of the diver.

Six hours of stillness,
Then I rotate into the black wetness
To do combat with the sea.

In touch with the mother-ship
By radio and a long umbilical cord;
I hang in mid-water, alone.

Through the metal hatch
I sense the power of the sea.

The Seven Flowers of Ballymun

As the flats come down in Ballymun we grieve
The loss as pain
But we're moving on to better things we'll never
Be the same
The old ways are going now
The changes come in fast
New houses, gardens, the internet
I can hardly recall the past...

But the children need more space to grow
And we need far more trees
So here's to the new town, Ballymun
Respect it, if you please
Seven special welcomes will replace the seven towers
The grey graffiti concrete will transform
To gentle flowers

We've always had the shamrock – but now
we have the green
The butterflies and honey bees are returning to the
scene, There'll be roses in the gardens to welcome
people home
And there'll be lilies on the windows to brighten up
the stone...
There'll be trees on every sidewalk with daffodils
at the stem
Tended by local women and nurtured by local men

Seven special welcomes will replace the seven towers

The grey graffiti concrete will transform
to gentle flowers

And when people come to visit they'll see daisies
on the green
With the iris and the buttercup – standing in between
They will see the highways lined with tulips
growing in the sun

That my people, is our vision
Of a brand new Ballymun...
That my people, is our vision
Of a brand new Ballymun.

Ripples

I came to your country ten years ago to work
I quickly grew to love your country.

I remember I used to love a place called Stonehaven
thirteen miles south of Aberdeen.
I remember I used to get up in the morning and run
down by the beach, and down by the river Carron and
sometimes I'd stop and run my fingers through the
waters of the River Carron and watch the ripples
form around my wrist.
I had everything I needed in Stonehaven then.

I remember I used to love the way the name
was made up of two parts Stone/Haven
And with your permission I would like to dissect that
name and take the Haven and leave the Haven aside
and take the Stone and compress that stone and cast
that Stone onto the pool of your imagination and watch
those ripples grow; up and out and into the River
Carron and down to the sea.

The North Sea and out one mile, two miles, watch
with me now, as we fly high over the North Sea
in a helicopter.
A tiger helicopter
And watch those ripples move out twenty miles, fifty
miles, seventy miles, one hundred and seventy miles,
one hundred and seventy two miles until those ripples
caress the steel tubular frame of a platform

called the Piper Alpha.
Watch with me now, as we land on the hellydeck and
move down the one hundred and forty seven steps
down to a place we used to call the dive skid, a place
some of you may not be familiar with. I remember back
in 1983 stepping backwards into the dive cage and
watching the Perspex bubble above my head and being
lowered ninety two feet onto the surface
of the water
Down into the splash zone where there were
jellyfish in every direction.

Oh that you could see what we could see!
There were beautiful colours, blue and green
and yellow and red
And long white tentacles moving down ten or twelve feet
below the surface
I remember being lowered one hundred and twenty five
feet into the dark North Sea
And at that time Occidental, the operator, had a rule
that before the diver left the cage he would blow air into
the Perspex bubble above his head so that the diver
would have a safety bubble at depth
I remember swimming towards leg A1 on the North side
And when a diver swims in the North Sea these days he
wears six thousand pounds worth of equipment
on his back and
On his head,
But inside the left hand of his helmet
There is a valve, called a mushroom valve,
it costs thirteen pence,
And if anything should happen to that valve;
if it should unseat
Drowning could be imminent.

My sixth sense told me there was something wrong

The North Sea burst open the valve
And the salt came in and stung my face and burnt
My eyes
I knew in that moment that drowning could be imminent.

I thought about my Mother and my Father
I thought about my Brothers and my sister
I thought about my friends
And I could feel a terrible slow weakness coming up
through me
And then I saw before me, stencilled in white
on the visor of my helmet
the words of Britain's great statesman.
Sir Winston Churchill said the six most important
words in the English language are Never! Never! Never!
Never! Give Up!
I turned on my umbilical committed to the fight
I pulled myself back thirty feet – one foot for every year
of my young life at that time.
I pulled myself into the cage and up into the bubble
And I knew in that moment that that bubble
was my haven
And from my haven back to Stonehaven.

We all live within striking distance of the sea
Tomorrow go to where the sea meets the shore and
run your fingers through a wave
And know that the wave is made of ripples
And those ripples came from afar
And some of those ripples are made by bubbles blown
by men working in the ocean deep
And those bubbles contain anxiety and fear and
determination and work.

And those men aren't just working for themselves
And the money they earn

Those men aren't just working for the oil majors
Who run the North Sea
Those men ladies and gentlemen are working for us
And the next time you watch your child absorb
Ripples of heat
From your North Sea gas fire
Remember to look at the pipe coming out of the side
of that fire
and know that a picture paints a thousand words
picture the men working out there
underneath the ripples of our North Sea
Think about those men
They need your thoughts

Casa di Copi

In 1992 I was invited to visit Romania by the Director of Casa di Copi No.2, the house of the children No.2. The children knew I was a diver so instead of giving me a teddy bear they gave me a furry brown seal.

Santa Claus brought me a gift
An airline ticket to bridge a rift
The best hotel that money could fix
Was orphanage dormitory number six.

A bed was made and set aside,
The colour green just like the tide.
A laugh, good music and
A furry brown seal
And a very original midnight meal.

Polite behaviour rules the day
Sleeping and eating and even at play
These boys are something to be seen
I believe they really are the cream.

They are led by Larenzo
Who is strong right inside?
He watches and listens and rarely has cried.
His music is special
It reflects a new hope
For tomorrow we'll wake up
And get up and cope

Written in the Orphanage 'Casa di Capi'
Bucharest, Romania 1993

Dedicated to Tezie and Laurenzo

SEÁN FRANCIS MARTIN O'DONOGHUE

Chop

*My brother Paul changed careers from being an officer in the
customs and excise drug dog unit to being a meat inspector in the
dept. of agriculture. This poem is about his change in careers and
the second verse are all extended family members.*

Pol O'Donnachadha

Cream is rises to the top
It might take time so watch the clock
But if your come from country stock
Sooner or later you'll face the chop.

Clane's butcher boys are in the clan
And Kelly's hooves here also ran.
Cully's cousins herded since creation
And Foxes well, they built our nation.

So now you down the mobile phone
And watch the herds you'll stay at home
You'll listen to no more constant static
You'll see a different kind of traffic.

Instead of finding tears and pain
Results of crack and speed, cocaine
You can use your knowledge and clout
To protect us all from foot and mouth.

14

The Purple Gown

I was on a FAS course in Loughlinstown doing computers when the class next door who were a hairdressing class chose me to be a model.

Cast the purple gown
Around the trainee's volunteer
Choose the model hairstyle
From the classes that are near.

Watch the silver scissors flashing
In hands so young and new,
Sitting warm and secure
Under a colour close to blue.

Watching a reflection
Of a comb against my skull,
With a razor poised and ready
To deplete a crop so full.

Like a piece of Wicklow granite
She gently changed the shape
From the crown whereon her fingers lay
To my neck down at the nape.

Purple is for wisdom,
She'll be learning everyday,
With her silver scissors flashing
She works as though at play.

Has Laughter Emigrated Too?

An emigrant returning home
Sits at night to write a poem
He writes of a pub's exclusion zone
On entering he was left alone.

The local people know he won't lie
Down beside them when they die.
Their thinking it is all long term
The native born stranger has much to learn.

And so he drinks his pint alone
Wondering where he'll feel at home.
The people sit huddled as home birds do.
Has laughter emigrated too?

The Homemade Desk

Five thousand years of Mayo men
No marches like the North you ken
A young girl smiles, provides a need
A desk on which to write my creed
It's wooden frame absorbs my thoughts
It helped her through the furrow's and troughs.
When for study and tests she prepared
The desk it creaked as though it cared.
I offered money, she declined
Instead she said to keep my find
And to send it back when I'd finished my lines.
Safe keeping a desk from County Mayo.
With a section for writing and a section below.
I'll mind her desk and remember her smile
When I sit down to write a while.

Written in Galway City, Ireland 1993.

To Do What I Must Do

The light is on in London
A girl is on the floor
She's deep in sleep and slumber
I'm wide awake and more.

My mind is full of urgent things
I need to do but don't
So I'll write while I am active.

If God wants me to waste my life
As I'm doing now.
Without a job, our useful trade,
Then I wish he'd show how
To feel useful in society
And not to live in shame
As it can be; to live with a drifter's pain.

I wish he'd give me work to do
So that I too, could feel sane.
It might be sowing seeds in Ireland
Or helping folk to pray
Or even feeding hungry children in the back streets
of Bombay.

My friends are all at Home now
Leading a useful life.
While I am drifting round the world
Not taking any wife.

There's Gavin and Porter, Pike, McMahon Too,
McCann, and McConnell all with jobs to do.
Not just occupations, no;
These men are doing more.
They're guiding and providing
Keeping wolves back from the Door.

My brothers too are working men
Not dreamers soft like me.
They will hold the fort in Heaven
While I join 'Na File'.

So maybe this is what's for me
To write and look and watch
And scribble down the things I see;
And find and touch.

If this is what is meant for me
Then I hope to God and pray
That I do it well
And say some future day not far into my life
That I gave something worth having
To the friends I left with strife.

The men who hold the fort at home
Are important men to me
And I want so much to help them
My Brothers, to whom I owe a fee.

But a man should live and be Himself
And give to those like me
Who go and search; and drift a bit
And spend some time at sea.

I've been away and Home again
And now I'm back and on my own

But I won't forget the friend at Home
Who didn't let me down.

It's hard to say it's right this way
But what I mean is this
Please God let me make my mark
And say 'There Lads, that's my bit'.

Its just like loading up a cart
Of timber, turf or coal.
I can do as much as any man
I too have a soul.

It's not like dodging work or graft
It doesn't feel that way
But I'm tired of doing work I hate
When all I get is pay.

Pay is good for buying Bread
Or going on existing
But me, I want to live this life
And not become obsessed with thrifting.

There's no joy in drifting back
For Christmas or New Year,
When I spend my days here sleeping
And my nights out drinking beer.

For a man to go to Ireland back
He must be living true
So help me please to find a way
To do what I must do.

Dark Shadows (Standing Stones)

Dark shadows on our land
In the inner circle all stand
Reminders of an ancient time
When natives dance to a primal rhyme.

Standing watching in silent places.
Casting shadows over mystic spaces,
They hold a corporate memory
Of a time gone by.

But in their presence we
Feel their eye.

Skellig

To watch her suffer
And gladly take her
place
Our princess of the Western Island
Race.
The glow Atlantic on her soft
white face.
Her spirit fired with celtic passion
And grace.
De Dannan held us in her breath
She brought us home
Away form death
To Live, To Love.

Written during a force 6 gale on a trip to Skellig Rock off Kerry.
Dedicated to Sorcha Conneely

Embryo Transfer

Standing on a farmyard
At the front end of a cattle crush
Watching the Veterinary Surgeon
Working with his hand and a steel rod
Removing the microscope life
From the sacred section of the cow.

Farmyard smells linger
Country colours dance across the horizon
Farm sounds play against our ears.

The surgeon works carefully, delicately
Manipulating the new embryo into the rod.
Joined solid to the beast
Up to his elbow in her so that
She can reproduce many of her like.
A pause to view the distant hills.
And then on to the next beast.

When the special task is done
The rod is rushed to be frozen
In a mobile laboratory.

The farmer watches patiently,
Used to the cycle of life,
Among his herd.

Verena, my Neighbour

36 moves in 18 years
36 new addresses
36 sets of tears
But when I move this time, I'll really be sad
Because you're the best neighbour I've
Ever had.
From the first cup of tea
And that smile at the door
To fighting the Druggies, the Landlord and
More
Our home was invaded by vermin and drugs
And we weren't aware, thank God they
weren't thugs
The Guards and their girlfriends knew we
Were at home.
But the young ones upstairs were shouting
'Pog Mo Thoin'.

It's not the fine building nor the glass nor
The chrome
That makes a place special, a place you
Call home.
It's not the paint on the ceiling
Or the mat on the floor
No, its more than that it's the
Neighbour next door.

There's a Hidden Place Inside of Me

There's a Hidden Place inside of me
That doesn't want to shirk.

A hidden secret part of me
That really wants to work.

Networking with the men of pay
Is a healthy way to save the day.

I can't help feeling lonely
When I walk to town and see

A hundred clear reflectios
Of that side of inner me.

But I love to sit and shoulders rub
With kindred spirits in the pub,

Accepted into the bosom of our community
By new friends

No need for isolation

For Siobháin O'Sullivan

*Written during a long period of unemployment in London
circa 1993.*

The Healing

I feel her touch
My eyes seal the warm mist of energy
To my soul.
Her presence moves with mine along my
Body
And I relax layer by layer
Until I touch deep sleep
Her love unconditional and radiant
Hovers above my body
And my spirit, resting in a cocoon of
Energy, touches her
I rest

A Description of a Reiki Healing.

Storm the Pill Box

Storm the pillbox
It's our right
To reject the medical profession tonight.

Hiding behind the churches steeple,
Protects the doctors from other people.

They choose now whom they take on,
And they dictate through (section)
31

people first, before some letters,
and never mind the phrase,
'Your betters'.

Written in Dublin City Ireland 1994

*The real pillbox is located in a kind of Fairy Fort
in the Phoenix park in case there is ever
is an emergency again.*

The Woman who Looked After Me

There's a woman who looked after me
When I was not at home
A woman who forgave me
When I left her child, to roam.

She watched me grow from boy to man
In a seat by the window, among her clan
And when she counted cups for tea
She always counted one for me.

When I broke her baby's heart and
I broke my own as well
She never ridiculed me
As far as I could tell.

Now I've left the high life
The money and the race.
I've time to reconsider when
Life moved at a slower pace.

I recall those long, soft evenings,
Watching Áine, out the back
With Marion and Catherine laughing
With Shea and Der taking flak.

I recall when Carl was little
And the questions he would ask
And his mother looking laughing
Amid some domestic task.

We used to eat digestives then
The coffee stirred with milk and sugar
But after we broke up
With coffee I could never bother.

We used to stir the milk around
Into the grains down in the cup
It's been twelve or thirteen years now
Since I gave it up.

But a gypsy woman in Romania
Told me to be drinking tea and coffee too
For even though you're far away
Sometimes they think of you.

I'm waiting now to visit
And to see them once again
You see, they're a part of me
And I'm a part of them.

Written in Willow Park, Dublin
Dedicated to Mrs Theresa Coffey

The Shop Girls

Standing to attention behind the till.
Watching the days customers queuing
Struggling with heavy loads.

Once in a while a smile will surface
And lift the air of burden from us all
I often take home her smile.

My Left Hand

Lay lines cruising down from the mount of
Venus.

Salt from six of the seven sea's
Cut deep into my hand
A long life line that shows
Children late in life
A naked ring finger stretching, reaching
to the world.

The palm criss-crossed by life lines
A tale of work and
The broken line of illness
Severing a career in midstream.

Its not a hard hand spoiled
By manual work or toil.

A fisherman's hand ready to strike at the
First indication of a bite.
A hand that can tie a bowline lifesaving knot
Or attach a hook to a line.

A hand that left its imprint on the sea
A hand that has caressed and touched
Manicured nails spell attention to detail

And yet a hand that can claw its
way up and out of depression

On the third finger a Claddagh ring
For hope.

Written in 1985 in Malaysia

Halfway a Teen

We have found no solution to this child's revolution
We have no time to pause to consider her cause.

For serious living can't be so forgiving
When the cries of revolution
Don't cause moral pollution
And you hear this at meals
As you enter your teens

Mind how well you have fared
Now your country's been spared
And the friends you have
Made on the musical trade.

You're a special girl Tezie
You'll drive young men crazy
With the depth of your knowledge
And your learning from college

And I see what you mean
When half way a teen
You're as quiet as a mouse
But you rule the house

Though not yet sixteen
You are already seen
As a lovely young leader
So many will need you

They surely do love you
Those women and men
And I'm happy to say
That I'm one of them

Written in Bucharest City
Romania 1992
Dedicated to Tezie

When Will they go

There is a place in England where young men
Are trained to implement British Government
Policy in our country
These men speak with a different accent to us
But it's not their accent we object to
It's their attitude
My poem is called
'When Will They Go'
The first two verses are delivered in the
Sandhurst accent.

It's bombing season so they say
Mustn't give in now Ho: Hurray
When will these terror types decay
And realise, this is not the way.

I don' understand these common folk
Their attitude to Crown sends peace up in smoke
But my men need training, we've a job to do
So search that house and stop 'Hey you'

The reply from a young Irishman.

There are two 'Ts' in terrorist,
Each day they put us to the test
Metal pigs daily scream into our streets
And terrorise with awful feats.

When will they go and leave Ireland alone

Then me and my friends can pack up and go home

When will they ken when foreign law's here
They'll always be searching for items of fear
You can't take a land, run off people and more
And expect to go shopping in your local store.

You act like a blacksmith forging iron young men
They wont bat an eyelid spending time in your pen.
You'll never defeat them, you never ever will
And if you keep trying they'll fight back and kill
You'll never defeat them, you don't even know how
So why don't you stop and give it up now.

For people are dying alone on the street
And prisoners are left standing all night on their feet.
When will they go and leave Ireland alone
So me and my friends can pack up and go Home.

Written in Aberdeen 1992

The Trust

Young People learn to earn a crust
at a unit called St. Vincent's Trust.
Based among anglo saxon names
Among legal paths and legal lanes.

Special people come to teach
To show them skills but not to preach
Beside Kings Inn the students pace
Their world becomes a better place.

Dublin city sends its youth
To earn and learn vocational truth.
The youngsters face life like a ramp
Here's where Elizabeth, has set up camp.

A life of travel, a corporate guide
Moving now with a different tide.
The days move past, each hour a prize
Teaching our children Entreprise.

For Elizabeth O'Brien.

Suma Ching Hai

A humble lady from Vietnam came into my life on the
7th June 1999. She brought peace of mind, serenity
and calm. My old anger is gone diluted and lost.
Each day she gifts my life with new improved friends
and I walk lighter on The Earth

Supreme master Suma Ching Hai asks very little of me.
Only that I meditate for 2½ hours a day, and
I refrain from eating meat.
Refrain from taking the life of sentient beings
Refrain from speaking what is not true
Refrain from taking what is not offered,
Refrain from sexual misconduct
Refrain from the use of intoxicants

My life is changed forever
A humility has entered my being.
I am attracting people.

The Masses

Safe Suburban Semi-Mind
We'd like to see but we are Blind
Sunday Morning in the Pew
But Property comes before me and you

The Day the Doors were off the Latch
Went out when Slates replaced the Thatch
We'd Love to See you among the Flock
We'll See you When We're back from Knock

Has Laughter Emigrated Too

An emigrant returning home
Sits at night to write a poem
He writes of a pub's exclusion zone
On entering he was left alone

The local people know he wont lie
Down beside them when they die
Their thinking it is all long term
The native born stranger has much to learn

And so he drinks his pint alone
And wonders where he'll feel at home
The people sit huddled as home birds do
Has laughter emigrated too.

Two Men Died

Two men among us died this week
They came in here, comradeship to seek
Things didn't always go to plan
But they came seeking; man to man
Each one had his share of trouble
But neither one was nature's rubble
Each was special in his way
Eddie and Peter had their lot to say
We made a space for them to grow
We didn't know how soon they'd go
We gave them tea and time to talk
We didn't know which way they'd walk
Their path ended a few days ago
Maybe we should watch each other as we go

With respect for Edward Tobin and Peter Moore

By Seán O'Donoghue
Ballymun Men's Centre

Sunshine

The screech of brakes
A red stop light
Stopped me in my tracks tonight
On a bike a girl called Fay
In her eyes sunshine and play

Colaiste Coibhín ag Staidair
Computers and the western prayer
Two bikes alone on the street at night,
One without and one with light.
Her name is one the Scottish send
Her home has given her for a lend
She comes form Cavan where the Rivers bend.

The Coffee Pot

Visiting a friends new home
No housewarming gift
No money for a gift
A quick detour into Brown Thomas's
And a full blown attack of Cleptomania
I see an ornamental coffee pot
That would suit my friends personality
To a tea

I swipe a BT bag to put it in
And head down the escalator
My internal radar tells me I've picked
Up a tail
I turn, too late.
The shop detective is kind
She hands me over graciously to the Guards
I wrote her a poem called 'Help'
The manager sneered

In my cell I walked and measured
The perimeters of my new home
For five hours I paced like a
Hunted dog until
They let me out
The Judge said 'Why did you steal a coffee pot'
'I don't like tea, Your Honour'.

Probation

HELP

The way you played your game
Displayed the gentle nature of your calling
To help those among us falling

Leave It Back

I fell into bad company
Bad company, good company, just company
They stole bikes, mountain bikes, old bikes, new bikes
I wanted one

One night when the moon was rising
We went to get me a bike
An old Michael Collins type bike in Ranelagh
I held the thick chain as my friend pressed the cutters
It snapped and I ran with the wheels whirring
in the night

But then I noticed something
Stop, a child's small seat on the
Crossbar, stop, reverse, go back.
Too late, what's done is done.

At home I carefully removed the seat
And put it in a bag so that
The child might have it on
The next bike.

Each morning I cycled to my
FÁS course, looking at the
Two marks on the crossbar.
I wondered was it a little boy or a
Little girl
It burned my conscience

After five days I decided to leave it back.
I carefully locked the bike to
The railings of the next door neighbour
And as I moved away the door flew open
And a man stood on the step
'Are you mad' he said,
'They steal bikes from here every night'.

'Yes' I said, 'I know, I took this one last week
from your neighbour'
'Would you tell him I couldn't keep it'
'Not with the child's seat'
'Tell him when I've gone around the corner'
'Ok' he said
The moon smiled down that night

Pauline

Deep down inside
A spark of beauty
Ignites her smile

She gives love to her small child,
Wrapped around her life
Like a lifeline to the surface.

Generous to a fault
She sometimes hides behind
A mask of aggression and anger
But Pauline the light still shines through

Fishing and Travelling in Ireland

Dangan, Rathdangan, Ticknevin, Allenwood,
Shannonbridge, Enfield, Digby Bridge, Ballybay,
Prosperous, Killikeen, Moy Valley, Athlone, Rahan,
Plassey, Rooskey, Lough Ennel.

Sundays spent exploring the roads and trails and
waterways
Line tangles in the early days at Ticknevin
Rudd, Tench, Roach, Bream, Perch, Pike, Trout.

The sun setting on a family fishing.

The smell of keep-nets in the car.

Abu 506, Abu 501, Mitchell 300, Matchmaker
2 pounds of sweets 'Devoured' as a family of 7 travel.
Each village shortens the distance to
Willow Park Grove Dublin.

For John & Teresa Donohue

I am afraid of Electricity and Spiders
And nothing else
(except injections in the palate)

Death holds no fear for me
For I did my best in life
And I will be reborn as a better human being

People hold no fear for
I have faced down the toughest doctors
and soldiers on this earth

Work holds no fear form me
If I'm not suited to it
I will move on

Love holds no fear for me
For I have loved and will love again

Authority holds no fear for me
For I am in contact
With the highest living authority
On this earth at this moment in time
Suma Ching Hai

PETERHEAD ENG. CO. LTD
'DEEP SEA PIONEER'
PROJECT

DATE OF ISSUE: 13/8

TRADE: DIVER

BADGE No.: PE 1050

SIGNATURE

NAME: S.DONOHUE

Seán deep sea diver's identification card

Seán sailing near the Mull of Kintyre West Scotland

The last picture taken of the wreck of the "Piper Alpha".
Taken by Sean O'Donoghue on board the Smit-Semi II

Basic Air course, Fort Bovisand Underwater Training Centre
Seán is sixth from the left.

Seán on the hill of Tara Co. Meath

Seán with Stephen on the West Highland Way

Seán on Board the Indonesian Tall Ship, 2005.

Lorenzo, the leader of the orphans in Romania

Taking the Strain

Racing from the North
A sirocco wind gusting
To each new white horse

Surrounded supported
Flanked, left and right
The soldier in him leading
To ease our mortal plight
Hard work has its own reward
He's earned the title Landlord

For Jimmy Quinn.

Two Dozen Mandolins

Smiling happy eyes laughed below the sound
The soft melodic sound of mandolins,
That lifted the hearts of all it reached.

The smiling eyes bring a message of
Hope for the people living in,
The changing soft underbelly of Europe.

Romania's best, watch us
Smile and relax,
And absorb the music from
Two dozen mandolins.

The dignity present among the players,
Seeps over the music and the language barrier,
And holds us in tight, like a fist grip.

The love the boys send out,
Stop many in their tracks and changes many lives.
Children of Romania, we love you.

Dedicated to the boys of Romanian orphanage
Casa De Copi no. 2
1992

Reaching for Skellig

The high rolling waves from Cuba
Set the scene for inner turmoil
And cut to the gut
As retching we dispell our inner waste

To suffer together and care and love
As the child within us
Cries for stability and a solid foundation

Like the rock

For Rachel from Barcelona

Naked Soul

Sitting in the Nude Café in Dublin
Sucking a fruit cocktail mango passion smoothie
Through a plastic straw
When a raw cold small brown hand
Reaches across a pine table
Towards my heart

From a rough Romanian Romany Gypsy child
Begging for change to help her change

Her brown eyes mirrored my poverty
But that day I was carrying
Two loose pound coins
One of which I pressed into her
12 year old hand

She nodded thanks and hit the street walking,
A blaze of culture

Broken Dream

Wood and Earth do not mix
Don't try to undo it
It doesn't mix

Torture, agony, pain with strife
Seek a fairer fire horse wife

Born in 1966 in the summertime
Leo the Lioness
Maybe she'll be dark with
Sultry eyes like the PD girl
At the round table at Busswells 15/12/2000
Friday party time
One big party

An emigrant returning home
Sits at night to write a poem
He writes of a pubs exclusion zone
On entering he was left alone

References to wood and earth and firehorse refer to Chinese compatibility circles.

My Inner Smile

One canine left, on the extreme right
So hard to smile, so difficult to bite
I fear to think, of that which I miss
That all important French kiss

Toxic crude dehabilitating medication
Called Largactil
Robbed me of a charming smile
A child shouts, 'mister you look so vile'

The Shane McGowan look
Has left me only fit to suck
And to cast my eyes right
To my disappointing luck

But as I sit and dream awhile
I can still feel my inner smile

Bardic Triangle

Hey you, stop and listen, check this out
Feng Shui for the mind
Were not selling
We're just putting it out and about
What?

No money; No honey
We don't accept cash
Only your attention and time
Listen to the rhyme

You wont read this in books
Strange looks
Follow if you can the rhyme
Of the man and the men
In the Bardic triangle...

Sean O'Donoghue

Stephen
Kerr

Seanie from
Killarney

Diagonal Spacing

I'm facing North by North East
You're facing your computer leased
We're learning figures back to back
Before today I was losing track

But now I've got my mind on stream
No time for poems, no time to dream
Last night I started off again
And studied with a different pen

I read the manual, and started notes
So I can do some legible quotes
I would have left and turned my back
'til someone stopped me in my track
Her dreams of moving from this town
I wonder did she sit at home surrounded
By Vivaldi's Poem

Written for Melony
A FÁS Girl 1993

Missus

Missus, let me mind your child
I raised my sisters clan – 5 boys
I'm sitting here all alone
Won't you share with me that
Feeling of home.

'I can't' replied the young mother
with a scold
my baby's only 8 weeks old
he's a gift sent me by the Lord
I can still feel
The Umbilical Cord

Witnessed in a Café in Parnell Street 1996

Washerwoman's Hill

He came from North Glasnevin
Where Dublin bury their dead
He came to live among us
With words spinning in his head

He can't do his washing
And he wrote some words for us
But now I only see him when he
Goes past in a rush

At first he wrote some words for us
Then he developed a crush
Then he wrote some words, to me
When I think I have to blush

I feel a bit upset now
And my boyfriend would be mad
If he went into my bedroom
And saw how many words I had

Sometimes I feel quite tired
Because I work a lot of hours
I wonder where he goes now
And who he gets to wash his clothes

When we met the words came slowly
'cause he's older I suppose
but I miss the feeling that I get
when he writes to 'Ringsend Rose'

I wonder what he wants with me
I date or two I suppose
Sometimes when I watch him
I wonder if he knows

He hasn't been in here now
For 16 days or more
I'll bet his flat's a state now
With washing on the floor

Dedicated To Joanne from Ringsend

Country Girls

All the country girls are gone
Back down the bog
Where they belong
How I miss to hear their song
How I wish I could go along

They leave behind a hollow void
And a lonely single man annoyed
But I can feel their presence still
When I'm alone with
Time to kill

For Dymphna Dooley
Edenderry Co. Offaly

Together

Amy: 'Seán why do you live alone'

Seán: 'I just do'

Amy: 'No, but why do you live alone?'

Seán: 'Well Amy, one day maybe I will meet a girl and I will get married just like your mother and father and have babies just like you and then I will be...

Amy: 'Together, then you will be together'

A quote from Amy aged 3

The Magnetism of Fionn Glas

Finglas has 26 pubs and 16 betting offices
In 1970 in new Ballymun 7 tall towers were built
No pub – no place for fun

Pinewood and Willow Park lay in between
With gardens and flowers and stretches of green

Before the Penthouse there was no place to drink
So the newcomers marched through to Finglas to think
But Willow Park residents refused to put up
With people behaving like Bart Simpson the pup

So they joined up together drawn to the call
They made a stand in Pinewood and built up a wall
If they are going to uproot our flowers
Then we will enforce the special powers

The Ballymun clan said 'No, No Way'
And they called in their friends the IRA
A bomb was primed, ignited and blast
And the wall in Pinewood became part
of our past

Willow Park called in the Guard
And though only twelve I became a bard
The pain inflicted by the decision
was harder for me than long division

Our people built up the wall again

And volunteers rose up from the men
But the 'R.A.' were quick like
an overflowing cup
And almost immediately they blew it up

The press joined in and called us snobs
But bicycles, cars and houses were robbed
The Special Branch went to the frontline
To secure the community I called mine

Without any fuss or load hurray
The wall is standing to this day
Today I see links with Garvahey Road
With a people refusing to do what
They are told

Like us they have their right
To stand and fight
To protect themselves from Alien might
But something was lost that day at the wall
We commited a venial or mortal sin
And by doing so we locked ourselves in

You see although I was only twelve and was
Taught by a nun
I also had friends in Ballymun.

'Love thy Neighbour'

for Sharon O'Driscoll

Moira's Team

Reaching back inside her head
To a cot of steel, a makeshift bed
Tots with eyes so brown and blue
Reaching out to me and you

Taking time to break careers
To go to a place so full with tears
And all the time we know there's love
Transmitted from the force above

We never felt so useful before
In occupations of bureaucratic lore
The smile you got from the child at play
Was all you want in the way of pay

It's nice to sit and shoulders rub
With kindred spirits in the pub
Meeting people from other lands
Special people who give a hand
Motivated by a simple dream
Meeting others who make the team

But when we're back among our own
Speaking here with people who roam
It's nice to sit and shoulders rub
With kindred spirits in the pub

*Written for a volunteer worker In Romania's Victor Babesh
Hospital for babies Dying with AIDS*

Magdalena

We have a teacher in our schoolroom up here
She teaches with laughter and
With smiles and with cheer
When the boys are all smiling at the end of the day
We ask what our friend Magda would say

It's not very easy teaching up here
But there's help from her colleagues
When often they're near
The work doesn't stop when the classwork is done
She's watching the boys now
When they're having fun

But when Magda's alone now
She thinks of her child
He's three years and growing
And soon he'll be free
To study at school and
To learn what to be

We want her to know that we notice her work
And her effort and care and her lack of shirk
We notice her daily as she goes about her task
Even when sometimes she has to wear a mask

Written for Magda a teacher
In an orphanage in Romania

Beata

We me through a double glazing smile
From a three-wheeled car that struggled by the mile
For fifteen miles she shared my time
Her red hair blowing as we climbed

Her red hair framed a laughing face
She moved with confidence and grace
She spoke of family and home
And as she spoke I wrote this poem

I say I wrote it, that's not true
For she wrote it between the forest and the blue
She wrote it every time she smiled
The verses grew as we walked the miles

Beata spoke of her husband and child
And forests and streets of her own homeland
She cried out for the right to live life to the full
Without the church and state creating a pull

Sometimes I watched her ascending a hill
Her words and expression moving in for the kill
And I looked at the sky and the fields all about
And I thought I'm so happy I really could shout

For God put me together for 15 short miles
And when she laughs she's speaking the words
From my heart
The sun kept on shining as we walked on our own

On the trail through the trees as we headed for home
When we reached other people the cold air came back
The end of the laughter
The end of the craic (fun)

I hope that I see her
That I see her again
In this land or her land or my land even
She brightened my day up with
The sun in her hair
It' funny that you meet someone
Meet someone and care

Beata was a Polish woman
I met in Scotland – she was visiting

We Stand Alone

(The day before Section 31 was lifted in the Republic of Ireland)

We stand alone as though in prison
We stand alone and wait and listen
Tomorrow night the ban is lifted
See how much the public drifted

Ethnic cleansing in the air
RUC and UDA a pair
For twenty years down in the South
The leaders clamped, sealed at the mouth

And yet the gentle people stand alone
Cleaning and washing with no wish to roam
Head down and working, supplying the state
Head down and working, supplying the plate

Supporting the family in spite of the yearning
They live independent with the money she's earning
While the tide of change spreads through our home
She remembers at once that she's not alone

We may never have to fight
To resolve this age-old Irish plight
If we get our request from up above
We can turn our thoughts to poems and love

But in the street where comes the light
Some will always go to fight
And if they go to fields of green
Who will they find, their clothes to clean

Who will they find, to laugh and talk
And forget about the Saxon yoke
Who will make them feel so at home
For who will they write that special poem

In anticipation
17th January 1994

Poison

There's some people selling poison
In a room just next to mine,
I met them here at lunchtime, they were really very fine

The girls are here for training
For a certain type of store
Where you go to buy cosmetics,
When you need to find some more

The girls are learning product knowledge
Pharmaceutical client care, and their
Learning how to speak with folk
Who need products for their hair

They'll help us when we're looking for
Toothpaste, soap and the migraine pill
But most of all they'll help us
When we're not feeling very well

You see their training covers grooming
And confidential client care
And because she can sit and listen
Caroline is halfway there

For Caroline O'Brien
Note Poison was a perfume on sale in a chemist shop

Twenty One Lines

1. The time is moving slowly now
2. I move from work to class
3. One day a week in Hebrew
4. and four days back at Fas

5. I'm learning about Israel
6. a land so far from home
7. and when my child is older
8. perhaps I'like to roam

9. It's February Twenty First today
10. My life's a quarter done
11. I've maybe sixty years to go
12. but today; I'm Twenty One

13. I have a job to go to
14. and I'm learning on my course
15. I've friends around me always
16. drawn by some gently force

17. At home I've got my little girl
18. and my mother's like a friend
19. each day will be a good one now
20. right to the very end

21. For Tracy on Her Twenty First

For Suzanne

When I give you this it's not a pass
It's an acknowledgement of the look you gave, lass
The look that settled across your face
When I spoke about the Aran place

Friend of a friend's friend
An unseasoned sleeping bag shared for a lend
Maro Polo No. 3
Was very special last night for me

To know you shared that special place
A friendship, intimate I see your face
You interpret Sue, the tree
And I interpret what I see

I didn't sleep but I read a while
Tomorrow I hope, I'll see your smile

Suzanne lent me her sleeping bag
She worked for Coillte – the Irish Forestry Board

The Rats

The barn is full of rats today
We moved into their home to stay
But we shudder when we see their face
But after all it is their place

A cut would welcome Weils Disease
The rats no doubt would not be pleased
For it would nurture determination
And with it complete extermination

For a rat can eat a poisoned pellet
But it has no ability to orally vomit
So it twists and turns and lets a cry
'I do not want to this way die'

ECO Moved into a barn infested by rats for a short period
Until more suitable accommodation was found

The Dole Queue

Shuffling, the crowd moves forward
Single file
Hands in pockets mostly
Looking down

Fifty pairs of feet leading to clear cut glass
And an anonymous face of a singularly
Public servant, dispensing paper

Queuing to make our mark, on society
In the line of artful dodgers
An occasional telephone bleep flickers red,
For part-time work
Hidden by the embarrassed owner
He pulled his acrylic sweater low
To hide the offending light

Poverty in motion
As the grey denim line weaves forward
A great equaliser, the dole queue
Ballymun, Ballyfermot and Foxrock
In the queue you are as one
A shameful statistic in the year of
The Celtic Tiger

My Front Teeth

A form of sadness has descended on
My mouth today
It marks an end of youth
A starting of decay

I lost four teeth which bridged a gap
Across my smile
One to a hard skinned green apple,
Another to the white sinews that holds
an orange together
and two to decay and the dentist

No more will I smile a reflection at
The World
Or balance my smiling eyes
Now there is only a dull plastic replica
In place of my living teeth

Old age calls, when the claw or tooth
Of an animal is gone, death is nearer

What to eat, how to eat
Learning to move food around the
Mouth to the safe areas
Not to disturb the false false teeth

I am left only with my inner smile

Charity

Planting a tree in Ballisadare County Sligo
I slowly dig the hole
As I part the tender earth
I slice a section of my soul

The earth it turns
And the worms they crawl
Before the autumn leaves they fall

Taking hold of the slender tree
The owner she named it, Charity

For Marie Gorman Paraic Larkin's wife.

The Foal

'Have you ever handled horses?
Here take this foal by the rope and hold him'
A quarter of a ton of muscle and sinew
With a totally independent mind

Glued to its mother with every step
And as the mare moved away into a field of green grass
The foal it jumped and pulled out the rope
My fingers slipped as its back leg
Came up with a dangerous hoof

The leg moved in a semi-circle and
Kicked out hard breaking my rib
On the left hand side of my heart
The rib where Adam gave birth to Eve

The foal kicked out in a horizontal position
Four feet from the ground
I dropped to the earth fast and hard
Gasping for breath, unable to find
Breath for four minutes
And aware of the oxygen time threshold

Gasping I struggled and thought of death
Until a friend turned me on my side
Later my veterinary friend asked me
'Do you bear resentment against the foal'
'Do you?'

Touched by Kindness

Touched by kindness
Soft display
Her eyes gave forth generosity
She shared and listened to
my tale
like an angel sent to comfort

from deep isolation
on a rescue mission
she sat and listened
to an open contrition
and accepted a soul from
outside a clan
who would have remained
an also ran

Dedicated to Deirdre O'Reilly

Friendship

Now there is love in this letter
And there is love in my heart
But I believe that friendship
Is where friendship aught to start

You see from friendship comes all other things
But I am concerned I care
That I'm often in your company
To see the wavelets in your hair.

For Bernadette Regan from Ballyfermot

Sifú Caraí

When Caraí moves across the floor
Both Sifus watch to keep the score
Her enthusiasm shatters
And the blows land where it matters

This leader of the fiery Celts
Is moving through Ed Parker's belts
You'll never see her coy
For it's sure she does enjoy
The suit that has no crease
And the physical release

She teaches trade and stock
With the hammer and the block
But Caraí's soft and gentle too
When teaching can be hard to do

So I watch her with an eagle eye
I absorb that feeling when I hear her cry

She showed me, life's secret's not in food
It's in that special attitude

For Caraí my Kempo Teacher
By Seán Francis Martin O'Donoghue

Visiting a Friend

She's a nurse, my friend, intensive care,
Devoted to work, no stranger to prayer,
Her busy schedule allows a window,
Usually on a Thursday,
I wait to see her and plan my day
Around her smile.

We talk and laugh and eat together
She loves another man in a western land
But she is my friend.

An Aquarian by birth, bearer of great wisdom.
Born in the year of the Horse, resourceful,
strong, extrovert and ever moving forward
She leaves me standing
A country girl with the soft strains
Of Waterford in her voice.

I listen to her, she brings joy into my life.
We wash dishes together and my work done.
She drops me home.

Another brick cemented into the wall of friendship

For Geraldine Shields – Abbey Duniry County Galway

Abort the Question

Abort the question, it's our right
To reject the journalist tonight
Personal views on the churches steeple
Protects our views from other people

Defend yourself and plead the fifth
Even if we create a rift
And though the words may weigh a ton
Remember, use section 31

Respect the individuals right
To struggle with the modern plight
Reject false gods and join the clan
And be a decent Irish man

The Empty Void

My room is the empty void
No one here to bounce reflections off

Only the window provides entertainment
As Glasnevin Cemetary Tower pierces
the sunset

I sit alone and focus on my buzzer
And wish it to awake loudly
To change my status and have company
Someone to make tea for
Someone to laugh with

Only the sound of my spiritual music
Caresses the void

The social welfare dole card lies heavily
On the table against a rent book

Somehow I have let myself slip
Into the quicksand of unemployment

I hope to dig my way out with
my pen

On the Run

I'm late, I'm late, I'm on the run
Too long in Stockport, having fun.

I'm 500 miles from where I need to be
I need a car and I need a key.

There's a garage there called Michael Prone
He wont mind if I take a loan

I've fifteen pounds for fossil fuel
This car reminds me of a mule

So in the window smash I go
Watching up and down below

The Yugo car was first in line
So I knew which key that would be mine

On the way back out I upset the alarm
The one feature I forgot to disarm

Into the Yugo and out of view
Before the arrival of the boys in blue

Away, Stockport, Chester and up the coast
Of my fifteen pounds I'd make the most

The only way to make more bob
Was to get to Scotland for my job

The fossil fuel I'd had to steal was part
And parcel of a Karmic deal

At dawn I reached the Highland view
On the trail of Rob Roy McGregors crew

And as I drove there changed the scene
To my second home, sweet Aberdeen

I parked my car like Suliman the Turk
And I made my way to my place of work

Two years passed by, and nothing was said
I thought the Yugo deal was dead

But I should have known right to this day
That Karma never goes away

A girl was hurt near by our road
And Belfast city was fit to explode

All men on our street were interviewed
When they saw my room I was pursued

My room was in an awful mess
It was upside down I must confess

Not clean and neat as I was trained to do
By my mother Teresa Donohue

I was asked what was my nation
And would I come down to the station

Now I was in a bit of a state
My mental health was on the plate

They worried was this man insane
Or could it be the northern game

So they left the lights on for two days
And questioned with the Scottish phrase

Nine Branchmen rotated as a crew
And one Branch woman she interviewed too

The reason for my swift selection
Was, they were afraid of an IRA connection

After forty eight hours of intensive light
They said now Sean give up the fight

You're not our man of that we know
So tell us what's wrong then you can go

What is it Sean what is the matter
Something's wrong can't you hear the clatter

If you tell us now you'll be off the Dole
It's good for the heart and good for the soul

So I told the branch the tale of the car
And how my journey had taken me so far

I told them of illicit calls to petrol stations
And I told them of my curse elation

And when they heard the make of the car
They asked me was I on the jar

Sean they said you're like a torch
Why didn't you just steal the Porsche

The Commander said he'll have to go;
Down south to England, down below

That's where he ran to beat the band
That's where he'll have to make his stand

So the cuffs went on
I felt alone
In the airport that had been my home

The air hostess was very nice
She came and checked upon me twice

I was shackled to a six foot mass
Whose humour could be awful crass

But on the plane he could plainly tell
That I wasn't myself, I wasn't well

He removed the cuffs, the pain to save
And he said 'Now Sean, wont you behave'

I laughed a t him and said 'Repeat'
For we were at thirty thousand feet

At Manchester station they rushed me through
They said his name's O'Donoghue

The sergeant gave me half a glance
He said 'Sean, you only get one chance'

The wooden floor of my prison cell
Threatened to make me more unwell

So for mental health and more security

I urinated a circle for added surety
And when they heard no cry or shout
Two of them came and bailed me out

My brief he met me at the court
He was a kind efficient sort

He asked me why I'd told the Guard
I told that I'd found the Lord

'A Christian man' he said intense
that will surely be our defence

And when the Judge said
'What do you say'
I said 'I'm sorry and if I may

Explain that when a man is lost
He'll fight at almost any cost

The judge he smiled and said 'I see'
'Fine – thirty pounds, you may go free'

As I was leaving he made one last amen
'I don't expect to see you here again'

Tiger

Don't spend £600 on a dress
Spend £90 and share the rest
There's a man walking barefoot in Temple Bar
No shoes, no food, no Mercedes car
He slept in a doorway for seventeen nights
Avoiding dancers and drinkers and bouncer let fights

He's humble, he's hungry, he sees you pass by
With Armani and Bally and your head held high
He could live like a king on the price of your shoes
Tell him you'll help him
Share the Good News

Don't breed your cattle on wasted ground
Hear the cry of the hungry, hear that sound
Vacuum packed steak
Is a waste of resources
Vegetable food can create far more courses
forty million people die of hunger each year
on Earth, many children cry in fear

Give food to the hungry
Give care to the poor
Don't buy a £600 dress
Like a whore

Think!

Ethel Alcohol

Outside SIPTU in Parnell Square
A middle aged man lies dying on the pavement
People step over him and walk past his shadow
Avoiding the pain in his dark brown eyes

His Aran Island cap stretched as a begging bowl
Containing twenty two pence and an English
one pound coin directing him east

He is bent double with alcohol poisoning,
Ethel Alcohol, although poisonous is deemed
By Government to be a legal drug

More people step over the middle aged man
At the other end of O'Connell Street
Two pretty teenagers hand out advertisements
For Irish Distillers

They are young and full of joy
And some of the people they give flyers to
May suck poison from one glass to many
And enter the growing ranks of alcoholics on our island

They may lie alongside our middle aged man
Begging for life
'Ah sure what's the matter'
'Didn't Jesus say the poor will be with us always'

Oceanography

Deep geography, geology, oil
Sucking fossil fuel from the bleeding belly of the Earth
No solution to petroleum solution
Catalytic conversion compulsory

Walk man, or cycle, don't drive
Get a job nearer home
There's simplicity in a walking radius

Air, fresh air, so real and healthy
Appreciate air
Don't live under a cloud of poison
Don't put poison in your body
Leave the earth at peace
And when the population reaches
Sixty Thousand – Move out.

Carmen: The Quiet Girl

Professor Carmen minds the class
Inside the rooms and on the grass
You never see her on her own
Near her's always a little one

I come out here in the strength of the pound
But she is vigilant all year round
I wish that she would be my friend
So words to her I could send

But she holds her feelings deep inside
And she makes me run and she makes me hide
Carmen moves with silent grace
And contributes love to this lovely place

She makes me feel so extrovert
And by comparison overt
She reminds me that Romania's biggest word
Is a word they call 'liniste'
(SILENCE)

Carmen was a lonely teacher in Romania

Drug Raid

Fear crept inward into the house
My neighbours fear affected me
We spoke of moving

The youngsters in the flat upstairs
Were dealing in heroin
Who were they connected to

The plainclothes drug squad
with dogs, gutted the flat upstairs searching
for more

Time has passed now
The youngsters are in jail
Heroin is but a memory now

Clan

I find my mind is more at peace
As I read and listen to guru and priest
I know that in another life
I did not have this pain; this strife

But like an eagle I did soar
And led my people to more and more
This life tells me that I am ill
And so I take my daily pill

But in the books, in the words they say
I read of miracles each day
One day soon my day will rise
And health of mind and body will surprise

Until that day I'll live alone,
Uneeded by my 'Clan' at home
To stay at peace with all that's true
I have my memories of you.

Written in Dublin City
1993

*Footnote: Margaret Kinniburgh was my last love. She nursed me
through severe ill health. I still miss her calm strength.
This poem is a prayer that the healing process will be successful*

Cruel Love

Cruel love started
With the man above
The fall of Adam
The seduction by madam

The thorns in Christ's head
'Why all the pain' I said
The four points of the cross
A child abandoned alone and lost
And the brothers to beat the Devil out of you

Where is the love with compassion and peace
The tender love and the joy of release
Alcoholic, Depression or Manic Pain
True love is the answer
It's always the same
How you love is up to you
But always be sure your love is true.

For Yvonne at the Botanic gardens

Little Girl

'Hey Mister you've only got one tooth'

'Yes little girl but I have got
Lots of money from the Tooth Fairy'

'Yea Mister but you've only got one tooth'

'Yes little girl
But really I've got one and a half teeth'

'No Mister you've only got one tooth'

'Yes little girl
But I am getting new ones soon'

'You look like a vampire'

'Thanks little girl'

The Tiger from Donegal

I've never seen a better face,
For love or beauty or childlike grace.
On St. Patrick's day at the 'Inn at the Park',
She stood alone, she made her mark.

Her guardian, a rugby rodent, tall and lean,
From another land filled up with green.
The China man matches us annually
God sent her here to be with me.

China says we'll bring out the best.
Instinct says to share my crest,
We laughed and smiled the whole night long,
China would smile in his home in Hong Kong.

But alas this red haired tiger is not like you and me,
For she was born across the sea.

Her smile comes not from Erin's Isle,
Her smile comes from a Mancunian child.
The Mancunian imperialist conquers all,
But not with fire or cannon ball.

She rules her world from inside her spirit,
To watch her play you can but merit.
I tease, I tease, a canine joke.
She's harnessed to no Saxon yoke.

She's Gaelic, Celtic through and through.
She's as lovely as the Nun that's blue.

She makes me want to go and call,
On the green hills west of Donegal.

God says you shouldn't love a Nun,
But God forgive me I love this one.

*Sarah was born in Manchester of Irish decent in the
Year of the Tiger.
She was studying theology.
I was born in the year of the dog.
And her companion was born in New Zealand.
In the year of the rat.*

Through the Door

Through the door
There's so much more
To stand in nervous trepidation
Waiting for the invitation

And then to sit by bog oak light
And say what will be,
Could, or might,

Of all the offices we
Might roam
This one feel the most
Like home

*Written about a publisher's office in
Galway City*

Scotland is Free

A Celtic nation gains independence
Highlanders raise their glasses of Glenlivet high
Picts smile and fish the east coast
Under a new flag

Blue and white cloth
Raised high on flagposts among the heather
The thistle is in full bloom today
Three hundred years of foreign rule, broken
on a summers day in 1999

The people are at peace
Rejoicing with one eye on
the North Sea oil
The people united and voted
An individual nation in Europe
Scotland is Free
Where are we?

Cherry Picker

The miniature crane reaches
Over the side of the ship
Stenna Seaspread
Steel wire rope lowers
Working tools to the men working
In the ocean deep

Coil, after coil, connects the frogman
To the mother ship
Steel wire rope can bite
And become a hangman's noose in
The deep dark ocean

The operator of the Cherry Picker could
Become an executioner with
The release of one extra coil

My friend lost three of his five fingers
To such a coil

Dedicated to diver Gerry Goodwin

Read the Book

Share the experience
Know what I know
Share and talk or walk

Let me share my joy with you
A book unshared is a dying thing
That could bridge the gap
In an otherwise empty relationship

If we read the same books
We are the same
If we read different books
We are different

Vive la difference

What!

Do you know you're on a bus to Finglas
The engine hums, people sit absorbed
In their own thoughts,
Working people, poor people,
Just people.

A nineteen year old girl sits
Lost in her imagination, gazing
At passers by.

A soft ringing purr calls from
Her mobile phone
She raises the instrument to a large
Round earring under dyed blond hair

And pursing the lipstick on her lips
He proclaims to the bus
Through the phone
'WHAT!!!'

An observation on the 40A bus to Finglas

Day Long Day

Moving through the day
With ivy and creeper
Watching the watcher
Watching the keeper
Minding our business
Minding our keep
Moving with a slow incremental sweep
Through the day long day

Written in Bantry Bay hospital West Cork in 1995

Support

I saw her
She smiled
She was lacking in confidence
And I wanted to help her
She spoke of pain and fear and frustration

I've done all that I can help her
Her throat was tight and sore
And she said she was not feeling
Good about herself

She frowned
I moved towards her and asked
Her if she would sing to compliment
My poetry reading

She smiled embarrassed and said 'Yes'
That night she rang and after a while
Said 'Bye Seán'

Dedicated to Mary Hasset

Backpack Waiting

Backpack waiting in the room
The world waiting to receive her soon
She's not quite sure where she'd like to go
To Saudi, Israel, or down below

A student of the healing art
Conventional pain an alternative part
Carlow calls each second week
Away from the parties, where new friends speak

One day she'll put the Backpack down
With a sigh and a gaze and a gentle frown
One day she'll settle in Dublin or Ballina
When she finds her own Master McGrath

Dedicated to Fiona McGrath

Milesian Blood

Milesian Blood (from the Spanish King Mil)
Coursing through her veins
Her brown eyes tugging
At the reins

A mariner from an ancient soil
Sent to reap, to teach, to toil
A guiding light before the range
Life now wonderful and strange

Dedicated to Rachel from Barcelona

Move Cu-Culainn

I am no member in this land,
Of group or party organisation or band.
Except for one on our east coast.
Where mistress and master learn to toast

But the lights went on in Dublin Town
To mark the Christmas season down
I stood in pain at Cu-Culainn's side,
And watched our culture take a slide.

No harp or gentle bodhrain drum,
Beat a beat of the time to come,
Instead our children sang a foreign tune,
A big brass band watched a red balloon,
Inside Ard Ofoig an Phoist,
I felt his spirit move my fist,
So I made myself, myself a vow,
Right here, right here, right here, right now.
In the year nineteen ninety four,
Cu-Culainn a tenant: will be no more.

We'll move him north by north north east,
In World Cup fashion we'll have a feast.
While Nelson's orbits time and space.
Cu-Culainn's strength will have its place.

If Dr. Paisley says Cu-Culainn was our first
B-Special: Then let him be special

What's With the Pain Man

Don't look into that hole
For in my eyes there lies my soul
Thorns in Christ's head
Nightmares in a double bed
I'm one of God's crew
What happens if they nail me too

Power dressers, men in black and white
Officers of the Roman Might
Deuteronomy says men don't wear frocks
Teach that to the Irish flocks

Lorcan

Tiny feet and tiny toes
Tiny face and tiny nose
Nurses work both night and day
Before the child was taken away

He sits with God in heaven now
He died prematurely, our heads bow
In the year two thousnad, two thousand and four
We can only hope for evermore

The loss of a child is pain indeed
The tears of joy turn moist our creed
His mother young and so will ken
To pray and wish and try again

'My tongue is the pen of the ready writer'
Psalm 45

By Seán O'Donoghue for Joe Barlow and family.

.

Lightning Source UK Ltd.
Milton Keynes UK
UKOW041912050613

211825UK00001B/54/A